# Bad Dogs

# Bad Dogs

## A Collection of Canine Pranks and Practical Jokes

Rick Stromoski

**CONTEMPORARY BOOKS**

A TRIBUNE NEW MEDIA COMPANY

**Library of Congress Cataloging-in-Publication Data**

Stromoski, Rick.
    Bad dogs / Rick Stromoski.
        p.    cm.
    ISBN 0-8092-3479-3 (pbk.)
    1. Dogs—Caricatures and cartoons.    2. American wit and humor,
Pictorial.    I. Title.
NC1429.S742A4    1995
741.5'973—dc20
                                                                    94-42755
                                                                    CIP

Published by Contemporary Books, Inc.
Two Prudential Plaza, Chicago, Illinois 60601-6790
Manufactured in the United States of America
International Standard Book Number: 0-8092-3479-3
10   9   8   7   6   5   4   3   2   1

For Odin

13

19

21

24

41

43

49

60

63

74

82

# About the Artist

Rick Stromoski is a full-time cartoonist and humorous
illustrator whose work has appeared in such publications as
*Playboy*, *Saturday Evening Post*, *Esquire*, *Harper's*, and *Good
Housekeeping*.

He has illustrated bestselling greeting cards for companies
such as Recycled Paper Greetings and Renaissance Greetings
and has been nominated for the prestigious Louie Award for
outstanding design in the greeting card industry nine times,
winning on four occasions.

Rick's work has also appeared in the CBS television movie
*Who Gets the Friends?*, starring Jill Clayburgh as a divorced
cartoonist. His syndicated newspaper strip, "A Dog and
His Boy," ran nationally in 1988.

Originally from Edison, New Jersey, he traveled west
and lived for ten years in the Los Angeles area. Rick and his
wife, Danna, and their baby girl, Molly, along with their dog,
Odin, and cat, Crusty, now live in the historic district of
Suffield, Connecticut.